Sharks

Don McLeese

Educational Media

rourkeeducationalmedia.com

Teacher Notes available at
rem4teachers.com

www.rourkeeducationalmedia.com

PHOTO CREDITS: Cover: © Todd Winner; Title Page: © Galyna Andrushko; 2-3: © Carol Buchanan; Page 4: © Hypermania37, LeicaFoto; Page 5 © Krzysztof Odziomek, Fiona Ayerst, Chris Dascher, Vitaliy Sokol, Chris Dascher; Page 6: © Diane Diederich, Dennys Bisogno; Page 7: © Fiona Ayerst, Thomas Pozzo Di Borgo; Page 8: © Photomyeye, Nicola Vernizzi; Page 9: © Andreas Meyer; Page 10: © Linda Bair; Page 11: © Michael Wood, Len Tillim, Btktan; Page 12: © Teresa Kenney, Ben Mcleish, John M. Chase; Page 13: © Liumangtiger, Dwain Tucker; Page 14: © Todd Winner, StevenBenjamin, LeicaFoto, Lee Pettet; Page 15: © Peter_Nile, Hypermania37, bamlou; Page 16: © Chris Dascher, Bart Coenders, Lucas Dawson, Chris Dascher; Page 17: © Keith Flood; Page 18: © Naluphoto, Vladislav Gajic; Page 19: © Sallyjogary, John Stublar, , RonTech2000, Ruth Peterkin; Page 20: © Ian Scott; Page 21: © lilly3; Page 22: © Andy Chia;

Edited by Precious McKenzie
Cover Design by Renee Brady
Interior Design by Cory Davis

Library of Congress Cataloging-in-Publication Data

Sharks / Don McLeese
(Eye to Eye with Animals)
ISBN 978-1-61810-115-0 (hard cover) (alk. paper)
ISBN 978-1-61810-248-5 (soft cover)
Library of Congress Control Number: 2011944406

Rourke Educational Media
Printed in the United States of America,
North Mankato, Minnesota

Educational Media

rourkeeducationalmedia.com

customersevice@rourkeeducationalmedia.com • PO Box 643328 Vero Beach, Florida 32964

Table of Contents

Chapter 1

Don't Be Afraid, But Be Careful

Do sharks scare you? Have you ever worried about being eaten by one? Of all the fish in the sea, many people are most afraid of sharks. This is because the shark is a **carnivore**, which means that it eats other animals. Most of the animals it eats are other fish. It even eats other sharks, with bigger ones attacking smaller ones. And, yes, some sharks eat people, but don't worry, this isn't very common.

Great White Shark feeding

Some sharks are only five inches long (12.7 centimeters) and weigh about an ounce (28.3 grams). The biggest fish is the whale shark which can be 40 feet

Whale Shark with diver

long (12.19 meters) and weigh 15 tons (13,608 kilograms). This is twice as heavy as an elephant! But the whale shark swims very slowly and eats plants and small fish, so people don't need to be afraid of it.

Did You Know?

There are more than 400 types, or **species**, of sharks. Only a few dozen of those are any threat to people.

Great White Shark

Tiger Shark

Bull Shark

Hammerhead Shark

In general, sharks attack only around 100-150 people a year. Your chances are greater of being killed by insects, such as bees, or by lightning.

Chapter 2

No Bones Just Sharp Teeth

Sharks are different from most other fish and animals. They have no bones! Instead of a **skeleton** made of bones, sharks have **cartilage**. Bones are hard and can break, but cartilage can bend and stretch. Cartilage is **elastic**.

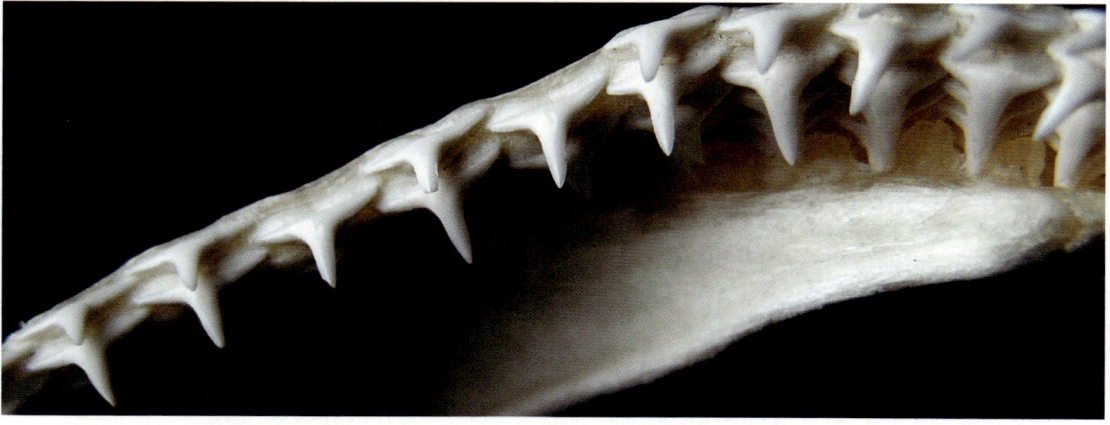

Your ears and nose have cartilage, too.

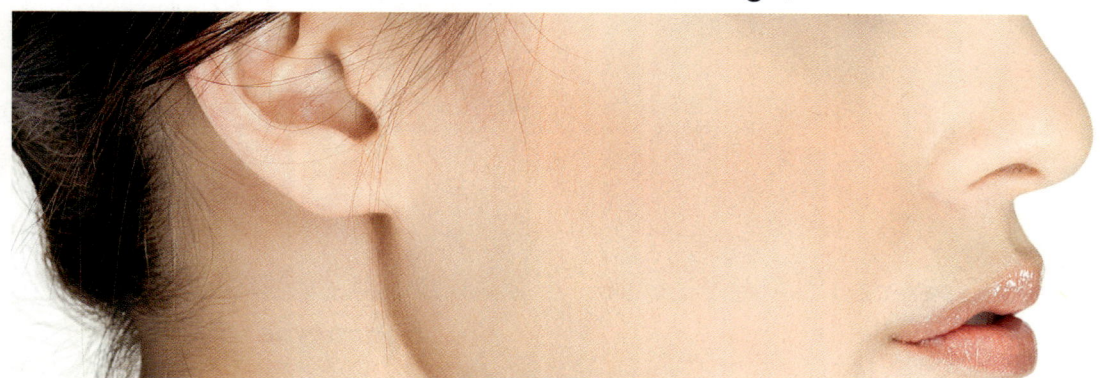

Being fast swimmers help sharks catch and eat other animals.

The shape of the shark and the way the cartilage bends makes some sharks very fast swimmers. The fastest shark can swim almost 45 miles an hour (72.4 kilometers an hour). This is close to the speed of a car driving on a highway. No human could swim, or even run, nearly that fast. The movement of a long tail provides the power for the shark. Sharks also have **fins** on the sides of their bodies. Fins provide balance and steering.

Sharks have sharper teeth than most carnivores. When a shark loses a tooth, it grows another one. A shark can have as many as 3,000 teeth at once and around 20,000 teeth in its lifetime! No animal has a stronger jaw than the shark.

jaws
and teeth

dorsal fin

pectoral fins

pelvic fins

caudal (tail) fin

Chapter 3
Older Than Dinosaurs

Sharks have been around for almost 400 million years. Even before **dinosaurs** roamed the Earth, sharks were swimming in the ocean. Because many of them are so strong and fast, they have continued to survive long after the dinosaurs disappeared.

Scientists have found fossilized teeth from sharks that lived almost 300 million years ago.

This chart shows the subdivisions of geological time, from the Cambrian period to the present day. In what periods did the first sharks appear?

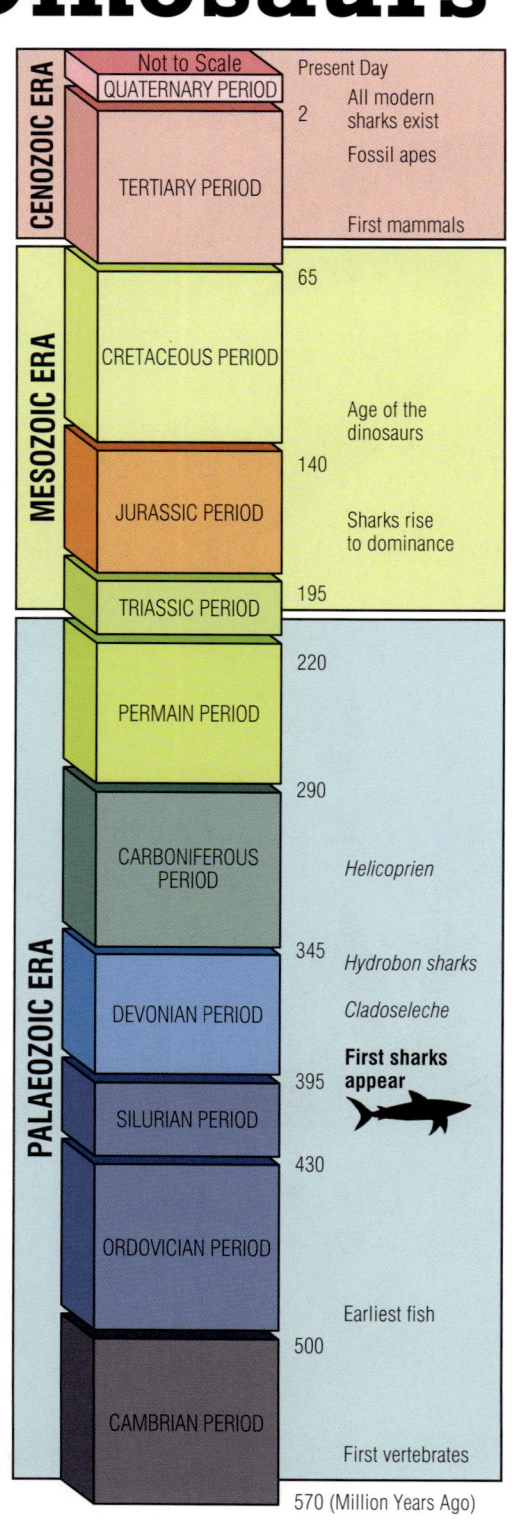

CENOZOIC ERA	Not to Scale	Present Day
	QUATERNARY PERIOD	All modern sharks exist
		2
		Fossil apes
	TERTIARY PERIOD	
		First mammals
MESOZOIC ERA		65
	CRETACEOUS PERIOD	
		Age of the dinosaurs
		140
	JURASSIC PERIOD	Sharks rise to dominance
	TRIASSIC PERIOD	195
PALAEOZOIC ERA		220
	PERMAIN PERIOD	
		290
	CARBONIFEROUS PERIOD	*Helicoprien*
		345
	DEVONIAN PERIOD	*Hydrobon sharks*
		Cladoseleche
		First sharks appear
		395
	SILURIAN PERIOD	
		430
	ORDOVICIAN PERIOD	
		Earliest fish
		500
	CAMBRIAN PERIOD	
		First vertebrates
		570 (Million Years Ago)

Some sharks live deep down in the ocean. Others live closer to the surface. Still others live in rivers or lakes that are connected to the ocean. Some sharks like the warm water found there.

Bottom dweller: Angel Shark

Surface dweller: Blue Shark

Where in the world do sharks live?

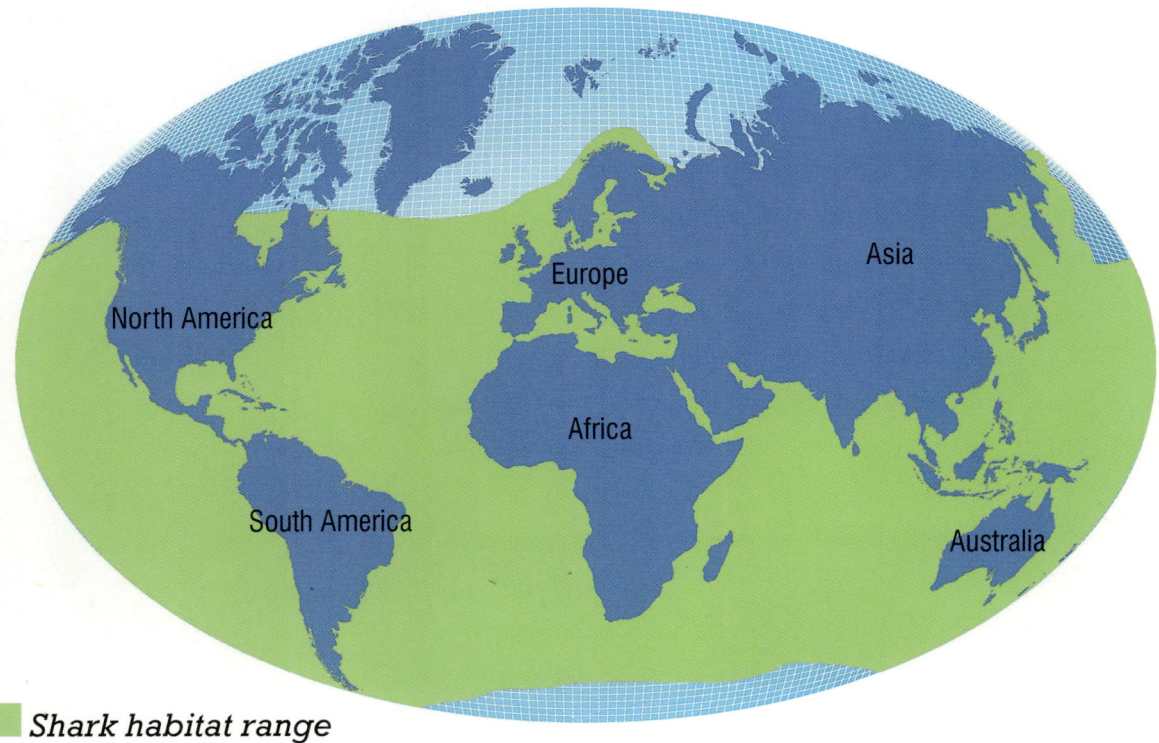

North America

Europe

Asia

Africa

South America

Australia

Shark habitat range

Chapter 4

Baby Sharks

There are many ways sharks are born because there are so many kinds of sharks. Some mother sharks have babies that grow inside them, much like humans. Other sharks lay eggs, like birds. Other sharks have eggs that hatch inside the mother shark.

Shark eggs

Shark babies are called **pups**. Once the pups are born, mothers no longer take care of them. Bigger sharks sometimes eat shark pups!

Blacktip shark pup

Depending on the species, a mother shark can have from 1 to 100 pups at one time.

13

Chapter 5

Sharks Close Up

Among the many types of sharks, the great white is one of the most interesting. Most great white sharks are 12-16 feet long (3.7 -4.9 meters), but the longest found was 23 feet (7 meters). Pups, at birth, can be five feet long (1.5 meters)! Adult great white sharks eat fish and other sharks. After a big meal, a great white might not be hungry again for two months!

Great White Sharks

Great White Sharks

Did you know it is illegal to hunt the great white shark along the coast of California? It is a **protected species**. If people were allowed to continue to hunt and kill this shark, there would soon be no more alive. The species would be **extinct**.

California

The tiger shark has stripes like a tiger. It is usually about 10 feet long (3 meters), but it can grow to be 20 feet long (6 meters). Tiger sharks prefer warm water in the ocean and usually swim alone. Tiger sharks do not look for people to attack, but they will eat people if they are hungry.

Tiger Shark

Tiger Shark

The hammerhead shark takes its name from its unusually wide, thick head. It has eyes on the side of its head. Hammerheads are about the same size as tiger sharks. Most of the year they swim in warm water near land, but in the summer hammerheads move to cooler waters.

Hammerhead Sharks

Chapter 6

Shark Scientists

Some scientists like to study sharks not just because sharks are interesting. They hope to help people with what they learn from their research on sharks. For example, no shark has ever been found to have **cancer**. Scientists are now studying sharks to find a possible cure for cancer.

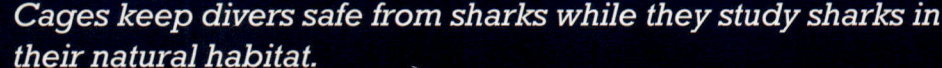

Cages keep divers safe from sharks while they study sharks in their natural habitat.

Many sharks are killed to make shark fin soup. After the fins are cut off, the rest of the shark is discarded.

The biggest danger to sharks is people. Some people hunt and kill sharks. People make clothing, food, soup, and other items from sharks. Many people are scared of sharks. They think sharks are dangerous so they think it is okay to hunt sharks. But people are more dangerous to sharks than sharks are to people!

Glossary

cancer (KAN-sur): a deadly disease in which some of the body's cells grow and destroy healthy ones

carnivore (KAHR-nuh-vor): an animal that eats other animals, a meat-eater

cartilage (KAHR-tuh-lij): a strong, elastic tissue in the body

dinosaurs (DYE-nuh-sors): large animals that lived a long time ago

elastic (i-LAS-tik): able to stretch and then return to its original shape

extinct (ik-SINGKT): no longer found alive

fins (FINS): parts of the body on the side of a fish, shaped like a flap, used for balance and steering through the water

protected species (pruh-TEKT-uhd SPEE-sheez): a group of animals that are similar, with laws to keep them from being killed and becoming extinct

pups (PUHPS): baby sharks

skeleton (SKEL-uh-tuhn): the bones that support the body

species (SPEE-sheez): a group of animals that are similar

Index

Websites To Visit

www.kidzone.ws/sharks/

www.sharks.org.za/

www.sharkinformation.org/

About the Author

Don McLeese is a journalism professor at the University of Iowa. He was written many articles for newspapers and magazines and many books for young students as well.

Ask The Author!
www.rem4students.com

24